EMBERS OF ANXIETY

by: abi lynn

Embers of Anxiety
©2022 by Abigail Lee

Published by BookBaby

Cover Design and illustrations: Ethan Main
Edits and help from: Traci Johnson, Ella Gibbons, and Carli Starr

ISBN: 978-1-66784-012-3

ACKNOWLEDGEMENTS

To Mrs. Johnson~

Thank you for everything. You are my light, my muse, my favorite person. This wouldn't have happened if it weren't for you. I am so thankful to have you in my life. I love you so much, Traci!!

To Rob Kalb~

Thank you for helping out with publishing this book. It truly means the world to me. Also, thank you for being such a good role model in our community through your service on the school board.

To my Parents~

Thank you for your never ending support. Know that I love you, even if I don't say it often. I am so appreciative for everything you've done for me throughout my life. I will always be your little girl.

To every teacher I have had~

Thank you for pushing me to be a better student, writer, and person. Each teacher I've ever had has made an impact on my life. I would not be who I am today if it weren't for you.

To Carli Starr~

Thank you for always being there and pushing me to be my best. I hope we stay close throughout adult life. Thank you for reading my poems, suggesting edits, and being a shoulder to cry on. I love you endlessly.

To Ella Gibbons~

Thank you for making suggestions and helping me through this process. Your book "Live Our Young Blood," inspired me and I could not be more grateful. Keep doing amazing things!

To Molly Warner~

Thank you for always being my number one. My life has been filled with so much light since you've been in it. You are a beautiful person inside and out. Keep shining. I love you!

To Ali Cain~

My best friend. My soulmate. Thank you for everything. I couldn't have asked for a better childhood friend. I hope we stay close throughout adult life. You will do such amazing things. I love you endlessly!

To Ethan Main~

You are an amazing artist with the most creative mind I have ever witnessed. You did an amazing job on the cover and the illustrations. I am so glad to have had you as a part of my team while working on this project. Love you, kid!

To my family~

Near and far, immediate and extended: Thank you. Your love and support throughout my life has pushed me to be a better person. I promise to always make you proud!

To my future self~

You did it. You are extraordinary. Never give up on your education passion or your love for writing. YOU did this. Be proud. I love you now, always, and forever.

AUTHOR'S NOTES

Welcome to my world. This book contains some language and references to some things people may find triggering or uncomfortable. Please read this with an open, clear mind. Feel free to jump over the poems marked with a "*" as they contain some actions that some may find upsetting.

Thank you, reader, for taking the time to explore my mind. I hope you find some comfort, see through the lens of a girl with severe anxiety, and understand that the world is not black and white. I hope you enjoy this collection as much as I enjoyed writing it.

embers of anxiety | abi lynn

TABLE OF CONTENTS

INTRODUCTION

my whole life, the voice i possess has been suppressed,
ignored and pushed away
constantly repeating, constantly restating thoughts, constantly
          defending
i am a quiet, reluctant person

i have close friends
few i trust
each one i cherish
and each sees the outside
while the inside is hidden behind a shield of traumas

i have a purpose
still unknown and unsure
but i do know
i need a place to expose my battle
to seek for a bigger purpose
in hopes it will bring myself and others peace
but there is no better way for me to express everything
than portraying a painting with words
that is poetry

my mind is like a playlist on shuffle
what will be today's genre?
a cheerful march? a somber interlude?
a combination of chemicals in my brain
that refuse to work as they should

my mental illnesses do not define me
but they are a huge part of me
a part that comes with me
a detrimental part of me
an important part of me

the only analogy that makes sense to me
is the comparison of anxiety and embers
how anxiety is the constant worry, the unknown
embers are the risk, a possible use of destruction, another
        unknown

i need to share my struggle
i need to share my side
i need to introduce you to me for the very first time
or my mind, if you must

i want my voice to be heard the first time
i want my voice to be understood
i want my voice heard far and wide

being from a small area
small voices are rarely exposed
although i have big plans, big ideas
all of which are being held back by my embers
the roots of destruction
causing a fire on impact

13

these embers keep burning

keep in mind that what you see is not always true
the inner core of a person is who they truly are
don't be afraid to dig deeper
look into the soul
rather than the color of skin
or placement of features
love who, not what

my inner world is still under construction
that has yet to be colonized
full of flames
of war
of peace

this world holds the embers
the embers of me
these are the embers of my anxiety.

EMBERS

embers are defined by the smoldering ashes of a fire
the still burning aftermath of an explosion
the unknown and misled coal of danger
embers are a cause of erosion
the change put into motion

embers are the remains of an attack
the gray area between fire and ash
the still smoldering rock
the fresh burning coals
unknown if it will spark a new fire or fade away

and these embers will burn and burn and burn
fighting through exhaustion
bursting even when burnt out
causing a new explosion
causing a new attack on the world around them

that is the scariness of this so-called anxiety
it's a never ending ember constantly burning
never leaving
the unknown
with hope it'll fade to ash

sometimes the ember is so sensitive that it may burst
causing destruction to the realm around it
it is then when I question

i question why my ember burns on
never fades to ash

it's always causing a new explosion
sometimes without warning
what is the point of living when you are just an ember waiting
          for the next spark?

SMOKE

i grew up in a home that was smokeless
my parents don't smoke cigarettes
neither of my grandparents either
a few of my friends parents smoke
but there was no exposure that affected me as much
as you did

you grew up in a home of smoke
and soon you took on the habit
your sweatshirts smelled so heavily of smoke
i fell in love with it
my brain associated smoke with you
the smell of cigarettes and the slight hint of marijuana
that intoxication was you

the smell now haunts me
whenever i see you, i smell it
i relive our time all over again
the time was short
but the memories are lifelong
and the smell of you
will forever mean so much more
than a memory of heartbreak

just by taking a breath in
it's so addictive
the sobriety i fought for

once again fails

and so

the smell of smoke will forever be bittersweet to me

because of the love you gave me

and the hurt you caused me.

LONELY

being alone is abnormally pleasing
for reasons i don't quite understand
nor will i ever fully understand
but an attempt to understand is the beginning of figuring out how to
be happy while alone

when you're born, you are alone
the lone screaming child in a room
filled with people who will never know who you are
even your own parent who would never dare to dig deep into
        the person you have become

i came into the world alone
my father wasn't allowed in the room and my mother lay
        unconscious
my birth was emergent so the room was full of doctors
and soon i'd find myself alone and far away from the people
        who were supposed to love me

i gave up on myself the moment i arrived
i was lifeless for a good while
soon became healthier
in fact i was the healthiest baby in the NICU

this became the first time i made a big deal out of nothing
this became the first time i would never fit in
this became the first time my problems were less important

than others

for every other baby was smaller and more likely to not make

it than i

because of my luck

and my health

my mother was shamed

because why was a healthy baby like me

in a room full of the dying ones?

like for the first time in my life

i wasn't enough

it is a lonely world

i have known this from the start of my journey

but my journey is far from over, unfortunately

but it is so lonely

you only live with yourself

especially if you live in your head

everyone else is either a figment of your imagination, or a

simulation

you only have yourself

it is uncommon to argue with yourself

you always agree with your beliefs

you are the only one who will ever agree with your morals

so then why do we make such a fuss when others don't agree?

what happens to you
and how things make you feel
can often be lonely
because you're feeling these emotions
but the other may not be

i've learned a lot about myself
and a lot of things i like to do alone
i love to read
and i love to walk
 or run by myself

this is mostly because
i can't compare myself to the other person
i can do what i'm doing
at my own pace

i prefer to be alone most of the time
but sometimes i need someone to distract me from myself
but other times i like to see what my brain can do
and things i can create

you are alone
with yourself
make your mind a place of your own, and live alone, content.

THROUGH MY EYES

i am looking but i am not seeing

i notice even when i say i don't

it's always the little things
the littlest amount of pressure and i'm crushed

my mind is like the golden snitch
moving at light speed
never slowing down

the big picture isn't so big when it is right in front of you

like one moment they act like they care
the next they're saying they're not ready for you
more times than i can count

in my eyes, i'm only spoken to out of pity
like they are never really interested
and that perspective drives them away

sometimes i feel like anything i say is not worth being said
because who is actually listening?
who actually fucking cares?

GLASS

relationships are glass
easily broken, fragile, yet strong and resilient,
when glass is broken is when it hurts the most
the pieces lay scattered across the wood floor
you were the one that told me to avoid it
so i wouldn't be hurt
but who knew the hurt would be you?

there's no way to fix shattered glass
you break it once, it's
unlikely to be fixed
sometimes you can fix
it with tape and glue
but tape and glue can
only hold so much
you are glass
but i dropped you
and this can't be fixed
and it's my fault
i could have held on
tighter
but the urge to let go
consumed me

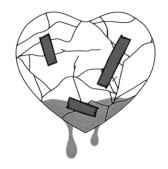

you broke me first
betrayed me, hit me
and i shattered on impact

this was over long before it ended

picking up our pieces

will cause more harm than good

so i'm walking away

to search for better, stronger glass.

THOUGHT: PT. 1

nothing i feel feels okay,

i just want to make it through today,

why do my thoughts always go this way,

they tell me go but i want to stay,

they never give me the time of day,

to figure out what i want to say,

to them im pathetic anyway,

please let today be okay.

SPRING

spring is a time of change
the transition between the wretched winter
to saturated summer

from ashy, pallid gray trees
to a blossoming, vibrant green
as the world colors itself again

the air turns sultry, sticky
the once chilled feeling turns into a crisp warmth
as the air calms down once again

rain showers,
blooming flowers,
earth's profound sense of new powers

a time of change filters in
as the world sheds its frozen skin
we begin to begin again.

PANDEMIC

eyes have become more beautiful
and meaningful
ever since we lost our smiles
to a shield that protects others
yet a shield that isolates our being

there is nothing political
about science
nor should there ever be
because science is the truth
and who holds office is a joke

the longer this goes on
the more i grow
and the more i realize
the things i wish i would have
realized before

the world is such a beautiful place
full of such ugly, greedy people
who take their privileges for granted
who lack respect for fellow humans
and they are making the world ugly

although the lives lost may be
to you only a fraction of the population
each person lost

was a life lost
and a loved one

why couldn't we have taken this time
and changed our hatred
to love
and acceptance
of others?

this was a time of pain
and it will reign on
and become a great story
to tell our children
yet one of the hardest things to talk about

more things were lost
than just lives, educations, athletics, social life
but a sense of togetherness
a sense of peace
a sense of being united

all lost because the knot that
was supposed to tie us together
was tied too loosely
and we are fighting
but the knot is almost untied

i never once thought i'd live through a pandemic

and i am not glad that i did
but if i hadn't
i would not be who i am
and i am glad to be who i am

until our smiles meet again
fully and not only half of the time
appreciate the eyes of the people around you
stranger or friend
and love them.

RUSH HOUR

my mind is in rush hour

during every hour

with traffic jams

and angry drivers

cars flying

crashes with no survivors

at least that is how i imagine it

but i've never lived in a city.

PURPOSE

i have a thirst for purpose
a hunger for importance
an itch for remembrance
a pain for change
i want to be that difference

my philosophy on life is simple
live
live like you never will again
to become important
to become that change

i don't understand what living is
not anymore at least
everyone else seems to be living
but i am slowly dying
i don't want to die
i want to live in a world
where living is free and fair
where hard work is appreciated
and looks have nothing to do with anything
where a personality shines brighter than anything
i want to be remembered
because what is the point of living
without leaving a mark?
i want to be known
without anyone knowing me.

YOUR INSECURITY

look at me
with your dark brown eyes
and faded hair
and tell me
you're not amazing
because a woman like you
strikes a woman like me
to be the most amazing creature
i have ever seen

your man is lucky
and don't you ever forget
that you are intelligent
and loved
your beauty is nothing compared
to who you are
and what you know

your brain is gorgeous
and your eyes are strong
everything about you is perfect
from what i see
and most times
i am not wrong

you have things about you that you want to change
but don't we all?

help me
and together
we can be the best version
of ourselves
that we can offer to this world

i know how unhappy you are
with your weight
and your personality
being insecure about your personality
is one of the biggest insults
because you're bashing yourself
for being uniquely you
and that is greatly sad

i'm sorry for your hurt
i only wish to help you
and make it better
to the best of my ability
just know i'm here for you
always and forever.

MOTHER BIRD

mother bird, your wings are strong
and your mind wise
your heart big
your beauty unseen

your mother hurt you
and your mind abused you
but you got through
and put it all behind you

mother bird, please smile
it has been a while
since i've seen your smile
and i miss it
so please bring it back

mother bird, please don't worry
i promise i won't leave in a hurry
nor in contempt or fury
because your little bird loves you
more than you'll ever know.

THOUGHT: PT. 2

i regret the times i've been quiet in situations where i shouldn't
i see wrongdoing everywhere i go
but i am silent
what will my words do?
will they help?
i like to think yes
but what if my thoughts become actions?

i walked past a lady who was videoing two innocent black boys
they were doing nothing but walking into walmart
she was videoing them and laughing at that
i really wanted to grab her phone and throw it on the ground
i wanted to scream "fuck you"
"mind your own fucking business"
i don't understand people
those boys were *innocent*
they were *walking*
i*nnocently walking*

and she was *laughing*
but once again my thoughts
were the only action taken
fuck. off.

AWARE

i am aware of the things i shouldn't be aware of
like when my parents are angry
not with me but with each other
when the tension is high
and no one in the house knows why
i'm sure you know what that is like

i am an empath
i feel your emotions with you
i feel the tension
so strongly it hurts
so strongly i can't breathe

i am an observer
i see and feel everything around me
the sensitivity on high
at all times of the day
sometimes unbearable

i am aware
of the things you have said
but i choose to not care
because i am not twelve anymore
and all i have is me now

at seventeen i have learned many lessons
lessons about life, love, everything

i learned who my true friends are
and the ones who would leave me for dead
a hard truth i had to realize

i've learned to accept what i like
but i still do not accept myself
for the way i am
or the things i've done
but i am still getting there

i am aware
more aware than i let on
so please be understanding
because i know
just how hard this is for you too.

BUTTERFLY

spread your wings and fly
away, away you go
to a better beginning
to start the better ending
colors exposed, dripping with saturation
fly away from here
never looking back on this world

butterflies have always been special
for reasons i don't even know
to me they symbolize freedom
remind me how i want to be free
i want to fly far away
i want to grow and bloom
without being tied down

fly away, fly free
and never look back
for it will slow you down
and so, spread your wings
my butterfly
show your colors to the world.

SHOWERS*

the water feels so divine
drip drip drip
the water spills down my spine
a sense of calm washes over me
i close my eyes like its therapy

minutes pass like hours
tick tick tick
my mind builds towers
creating stories, conversations, confrontations,
my mind forces accusations

a razor slides across my thigh
deep deep deep
the pain creates a high
my mind goes blank feeling numb
i silently promise myself this is the last one

it hurts but i tell no one
hush hush hush
what if they tell someone
i can't take the look of worry
i dry off in a hurry.

THIS BODY*

this body does not belong to me
i am not who i see
for i feel different
i am not who i look like
and that hurts

i have a desire to hurt myself
for what i am not sure
but i feel the need to
torture my body
and my mind

my head has made my life hell
the environment around me
has no effect
it is all in my head
and that is a fact

i created this world
and this world is scary
i am living your worst nightmare
i take your pain
and put it on me

i carry the weight of others
because i am not strong enough
to carry my own

even looking at the weight
is exhausting

i would rather hold all of your feelings
than hold my own
i would rather help you
than help myself
it is my way of coping

i am unhealthy with coping
i say i can't destroy myself this way
but in another way instead
because it will hurt less

cut at the skin level
enough for it to bleed
but not enough to bleed out
enough to leave a mark
but not enough to leave a scar

this body has become an art piece
painted over time and time again
this face is only a canvas
this body needs a new coat
please accept me when i am painted again.

NIGHTTIME *

the nights are the worst
and they always have been
i feel the urge to cut at night
i go insane in the night time
most nights, anymore, i cry myself to sleep

it's when the paranoia sets in
when the mistakes of the day shine brightest
when my mind moves its fastest
when i think about you
and how much i fucked up
when i think about life
and how i will fuck it up

i think about my dream
will it be another nightmare?
what is to happen tonight while i am sleeping?
how many times will i wake up tonight?

the nights are always so awful
because i hurt myself most nights
locked alone and trapped in my own head
i can't breathe
and i start to not want to breathe
i can't breathe
it's so hot in here
i rip my shirt off

and i lay there
trying to tear my hair out

shaking unbelievably hard
rolling while tears stream down my face
while my headphones blast music
that promotes sadness
or really upbeat music
as an attempt to catch up to my brain

and while you may laugh at the fact
that i listen to sad music when i am sad
you're wrong
because i wasn't sad
i made myself sad

except it wasn't me
and it wasn't my decision
i didn't want to do this to myself

my cuts burn so bad
but my skin is clear
until i unveil those cuts
by pressing my knife to my skin
and once again letting myself exhale
because the damage is done

and i can finally sleep

only to wake up again
live another day
and until night falls again
and my nightly attacks
become a nightly routine.

DO YOU REALIZE THIS IS WHAT HAPPENED TO YOU?*

i remember that night
like it was just a couple of hours ago
the room brisk
the sheets warm
your body slamming itself against mine
the unease of the pressure
and the feeling of fear

my mind had been gone
and you were there
taunting me
telling me
i should let you in
i should allow you in
and if i didn't you wouldn't talk to me
anymore

and so when the lights went out
i let you in
guided you to the room
where we looked into each other's eyes
in yours i saw nothing
but poison and contempt
it was then when i realized
this was a mistake

the next thing i know

you're in the small bed with me
just laying
and i'm screaming
"leave"
but the only thing heard
is the sound of our breaths

you kissed me first
hard, so hard it hurt
it was neither sweet nor warm
but cold and bitter
"i didn't say yes to this," i thought

you're on top of me
and i'm unable to move
is this a dream? or am i just imagining this?
you're heavier than me, stronger than me
on top of me
gripping my wrists with your hands
as your hips thrust into mine
my mind is numb

i'm frozen
i tell you to stop
and you do, for just a moment
and then you continue
to slide off my pants
a reluctant thought appears

"maybe i need this. maybe this is okay"
but it wasn't

the next thing i remember
is pressure and a slight pain
i'm not enjoying a minute of it
you slide into me roughly with your fingers
it's like you think i like it
but inside i'm crying
as your pushing and shoving
i just lay there
staring at the ceiling
while you rock your body all over mine
as if i'm a pillow in your bedroom
"please.. stop"
but you don't

you roll me over and i'm on top
you tell me what to do
and as if i'm being told by a drill sargent
 i do it
and i tell you
"i guess i'm yours now"
something i felt forced to say

you were kind enough to ask
if i wanted to do full intercourse
but i told you i'm tired

"but you know you want to," you say

no i don't

i want you to leave

you suggested without protection

and i profusely said no

but you wouldn't give up

eventually, i convinced you it was late

i had to work in the morning

"next time, i'll bring condoms," you say

as if there will be a next time

you left

i went back to the bed

i laid down and closed my eyes

tears burning my cheeks

my hips sore and most likely bruised

"it was just a dream," the voice said

"this is what you wanted," it screamed

"you let him in. that is all. your. fault," and i believed it

there was a time when i considered you to be the victim

as if i were the one

luring you in

that i took advantage of you

in fact i didn't even call it "assault"

until i was told

"did you realize this is what happened to you?"

TAKEN ADVANTAGE

too much too much
"a woman is too much"
too emotional or too opinionated
we eat too little or too much
we dress too little or too much
no woman is ever enough for anyone

a woman is a strong soul
stronger than all
a creature with so much potential

she feels emotions and expresses them so you can understand
        them
don't take advantage
she wears revealing clothes so she can blossom out of her
        comfort zone for **herself**
don't take advantage
she fights for her rights because her say is equally as important
don't take advantage
she's fighting a battle you can't see so don't bother her
don't take advantage
a woman is a human

how can a man think that a woman is an object
when we are constantly beating the odds?
a woman paves her own way
she earns her living through the discrimination

takes in all the hate

but fights for herself and her rights

she chooses herself for her

with no comment from any man

no help from any man

don't take advantage.

THOUGHT: PT. 3

everything i say is taken out of context
*i didn't mean it like tha*t
i promise i didn't
i speak too soon or too late
words are so difficult
i say things i don't really mean
that is the worst thing about me

i don't hate
or i try not to hate
i just convince myself that others hate me
i am a master at self-depreciation.

HATE ME

hate is a strong word
but my insecurities are stronger
and it makes me feel as if
my flaws are on display for you to see
and you hate them too

by looks i have a tendency to not be liked
i'm too quiet
i rarely speak out
and i've been told this trait is despised
i hate talking loud
and drawing attention to myself

i have a unique style
with tattoos and heavy jewelry
half a shaved head
and i dyed my hair red
it's a vibe not many traditionals enjoy
even as the world progresses

people think i'm being rude when i don't talk
it's not that i don't want to
and it's not purposeful
i sit back and listen
i am an observer

i see things happen

i watch because i'm too scared to do
but it is better to not be involved
and i'm the quiet type
some people despise that

you misunderstand me
you don't know me
so you can't hate me
that is my job.

I HATE THE STRESS OF MY FRIENDS

don't get it twisted
it's not true
i don't hate them
i just struggle to accept
that they accept me

i have amazing friends
they are my loves, my light
i'd do anything for them
in an instant

i tend to put them first
to me they come first
but i'm trying to change that
because it's not working

opinions differ
and values change
friendships fade
new ones form

i know i am loved
but i feel hated
but i love them
and i hate them

my closest friends

the ones who know me
never give up on me
they are "the ones"

the one who reciprocates
she gives me the utmost amount of love
she doesn't judge and is honest
she is my healthiest friendship

the one who has faded
she was by my side through the worst
but pushed away during the fall
she is my most memorable friendship

the one who is my person
my forever, my soulmate, my polar opposite
no matter what she has never left
she is my longest friendship

the one who crashed into my life
he showed up at my worst
and presented to me the best
he is my easiest friendship
those four are the ones
who i am closest to
the others are people i cherish
whom i adore
and nothing could ever change that

they are my people

options are limited and people are few
i grew up with these people
and i know all of these people

small town friendships are hard
because it is harder to explore
it is harder to find a variety of people
to call yours

i chose these people because i love them
when i hate them because i feel they hate me
i love them with all my heart
but i hate them.

SEVENTEEN

i don't recognize myself
this body that was once small
and pure
and loveable
is no longer so
small
or pure
or loveable

from little girl to young woman
i've always dreamed of being
little me sits on her bed
dreaming of this girl
who is supposed to be happy
supposed to be confident
supposed to look older

i still see my child face in me
i can't understand why so many people
think i am older than i am
while i'm not offended,
i'm just overwhelmed
because i don't know if i want to grow up

the future scares me
and for my whole year of seventeen
the future has been the main conversation

57

it is like everyone expects you to know
exactly what you want to do next
but i am just trying to make it
through the day

my year of seventeen
started in quarantine
because my mom got covid
and so i spend the first two weeks
in this new age
isolated

everything seemed to get worse from there
my birthday is in september
and in february i became weak
my mental state took a drop
and it hasn't gotten much better since

i relapsed after three years
something i never thought i would do
but the pain got so bad in my head
i thought inflicting it on myself
would relieve it
and, boy, i was wrong

i still have so much more learning to do
about this whole thing called life
i have so much more to say

and i have so much i want to do
the year of seventeen has taught me
what these wants are

i came to so many realizations this year
and in such a short time
and in not so long i will be
becoming a new age
the age of eighteen
and that thought terrifies me
because the child i once was
no longer exists

if there is one thing i would want to take from seventeen
it would be to remember this struggle
and fix it, not with tape and glue
and to be more accepting and honest towards myself
because in this age and in every age
that is the most important thing.

RELIGION

i'm not a religious person
i grew up in a home
full of love and faith
but faith is not something
i've really ever connected with

there is guilt in this
believe it or not
but this guilt is not strong enough
to make me go back
and start to believe

they say i'll find it one day
and maybe that is so
but i don't foresee it happening
and thats okay
it really is okay

what i don't understand
is how humans subject to a higher power
a creature unknown
and still love it unconditionally
it's something i never understood

in my mind your higher power is you
put you above everything
for most of the time

61

and maybe then you'll find peace
and you'll be happy

but we humans are insecure
putting ourselves first is not what we do
it's not something we enjoy doing
but it truly is an amazing thing
have you ever tried it?

happiness is not provided my a higher being
we are the higher being
you are a higher being
religion shouldn't matter
if this is so.

GUILT

i have it easy
my parents take care of everything
and i'm often reminded of that
i have no worries, no nothing
and the brain in my head
can be so easily changed
at least that is what you said

i'm tired of your guilt trips
i know you're struggling too
and i feel awful
i do
but as you always remind me
you are the parent
so please be one

i'm not ungrateful
and i thank you for everything
i take nothing for granted
i promise
because you taught me not to
and for that i'm grateful

we have such different opinions
most you think are influenced

but surprise

i have a brain and emotions and opinions

i am not just an object

i deserve to be seen and heard

for once.

THINKING PROBLEM

some people have a drinking problem
i have a thinking problem
and this thinking problem becomes a drinking problem
i don't want to be sober anymore

except i don't want to drink
because when i drink i think
but when i don't drink i think
there is no place safe anymore

what is the point of living
there are so many problems with living?
this life is not very giving
i don't want to live here anymore.

FIRST LOVE

i feel incapable of love
for no one has loved me
the same way i have loved them
and no one has seen me
the way i see them

i am a fast faller
a free faller
but i ruin it so quickly
so early
i never even get a chance

i remember my first love
blonde hair, dreamy eyes
a soul so beautiful
a boy so misunderstood
and i loved him

i see him every day
in the hallway
sometimes in my dreams
there is not a day that goes by
when i don't think of him

he was a good one
one i wanted to keep
but all i have now

is memories
and love anxiety.

THOUGHT: PT. 4

i have always been one to silently rebel
i never cared if i swore online
i went against most of what my parents said
i never thought the way others think
i've always been different

my parents never worried about me
i was supposed the be the one
to get it all right
and i feel i failed them
as one does
when expected to succeed

the past year has been hard
and the media coverage of it all
is sickening and exhausting
when will it end?
the mindless beats at each other

i want to stand out and protest
i want to stand up for the ones
who cannot
i want to go against the normal and fly
fly free and fly high.

LOST

my mind is drained and dry
the juices have spilled out
and there is nothing left to be spilled
at a loss for everything
and for everyone

i am burnt out
both mentally and physically
all that is left is the structures
from the fire
i feel exposed

i can no longer function
i am out of order
waiting for a mechanic
to be sent my way
but i'm losing hope.

I MISS YOU

i'd be lying if i said i didn't miss you
everything about you was perfect
and i ruined it
like everything else
i wanted to love you
and for you to love me
but everything gets so much more complicated
when love is involved.

I LOVE YOU

i will never stop loving you
i have loved you forever
ever since i laid eyes on you
and i will never not love you
because you are you

i will never tell you i love you
because the words will never come out
and i know how frustrating that is
it frustrates me too
but i can't tell you "i love you"

i just want to love you for the rest of my life
and i never want to say goodbye
for the rest of my life
i want you by my side
because i love you.

CRUSH

i really tried
reading you like a book
but i couldn't get through a page
i read and i read
but the page was blank
and your face was
the only thing i could
make out

your voice intoxicates my soul
and your eyes strike my heart

this love is a dangerous game
and i hate playing games
but you're so worth it
oh, you're my purpose
i want to keep you in
my circle

but you don't know my name
and you don't know my story

i see the way you look
at yours
and i want to be yours
i never want to give up on you
but i feel like i really need to

it's driving me insane

but i'll never tell you my name.

STAR SHOPPING -LIL PEEP

there are few songs in the world
that i never get tired of hearing
this is one of them

the intensity of this song
it is almost unbearable

it pulls me in every direction
pulling at my heartstrings

my mind wonders
into the universe
unfolded by the melody

"look at the sky tonight
all of those stars have a reason
a reason to shine
a reason like mine
and i'm
falling to pieces"

powerful
and immensely heart wrenching

so complex
yet so simple

i'm so broken
over the lyrical movements

a fragile feeling
like i'd break at any second
just like the stars

rest in peace, peep
thank you for giving me the stars.

I WANT TO HOLD YOUR HAND

not out of love or affection
but out of fear and agitation
because walking through this life
especially alone
is extremely terrifying

i want you to place your hand in mine
and guide me
tell me what to do
tell me how to do it
because i don't think i can do this
alone.

IN MY MOMENTS WITH YOU

in my moments with you
i would study your eyes
i would run my hands through your hair
and my fingers across your lips
my head on your chest
feeling your heartbeat
i would feel your hands
your cold, cold hands
soft and a perfect fit to mine

i held your face in my hands
your facial hair making your face rough
as our lips collided
gentle and easy
breathing in each other's air
warm and sweet
when i knew i was saying goodbye
i made sure to memorize your face
to remember how your hair felt
to hold your gaze
i wanted to make sure
that i wouldn't forget

yet my mind was already in my car
i was already out the door
while you were standing in front of me

i will never forget the look on your face

so beaten down and sad

how i held you with your head on my chest

your arms around my waist

sitting in a thick silence

tears fell down my face

how i never wanted that moment to end

because now it is only a memory.

ROSES

in a room full of red roses

i want to be a white rose

because it is simple and pure

not that i am simple nor pure

but i have a desire to be

i have a desire to stand out while blending in

i want to be extraordinary

and not share it

not to be selfish

but to be me

without judgment

from myself

or others.

CIRCLE OF LIFE

the circle of life is theoretically nonexistent
there is no such thing as a circle of life
a life is a line
beginning to end
you only live once

they say calm comes before the storm
but there is also a calm after the storm
coming down off of that high
there is a moment of silence
a calm
that is the circle
the circle of events

there is a circle in every life instance
except for life itself
life has ups and down constantly
violently
but it is no circle

your ends will never meet
you'll never end up where you started
embrace the calm inbetween the storm
and burst from your enclosed circle.

SEXUALITY

i was raised in a straight mindset
because i grew up in a catholic home
and a man and a wife are the only
real family that can form

i have never truly believed that
nor will i ever believe that
because i like women
and i like men
and either can be the ones
i end up with

sexuality isn't a game
and it isn't something taken lightly
it is something sacred
and something terrifying

the thought of anyone finding out
that i have an attraction to girls
is mortifying
only because of the environment i grew up in
and that angers me

i am bisexual
i love men and women
and i am okay with that
and i want to be okay with that

because women are amazing
yet so are men

i have only kissed men
so i don't know for sure
but i think i should experiment
because i feel that is only right

i am tired of lying to myself
if i know i am something
why can't i just accept it?
because if i'm judged
why should i care?
because i do

i don't want to be ashamed
and i honestly don't think i am
i am just scared of what people will think
or if i'll be accepted by my own family
and that is terrifying to me.

RELAPSE

the easiest thing to do is to give up

and let go

even when you know

you could have held on for so much longer

but you decided to take the easy route

once again

destroying the progress you've made

but then you begin to think

was it even progress at all?

or just time to let the scars heal

that is what relapse is

you give in the the hurt

you give in to the torture

weighing on your mind

because you start to think

you are not as strong as you once were.

THOUGHT: PT. 5

don't get mad if you think
a poem is about you
because you're probably right
and you should be honored
that i took the time
out of my day
to even spare you
a single thought.

PACKING MY BAGS

i am packing my bags
suitcase full of memories
and a carry on with my sorrow

i am going away
from you
my poison

the uncertainty you give me
is most unbearable
and the pain piercing

you stuck your claws in my back
causing the faintest
yet most harrowing wounds

and for years i stood by you
best friend
the title i felt forced to say

i am sorry i bore you so much
and to you it is whatever
but now i am packing up
and moving on
to bigger
and better things.

THE DIVIDED STATES OF AMERICA

it seems like the only thing people see the same these days are
       the clouds in the sky
because the sky is the thing each and every one of us sees
       when we look up
i think that is the only thing we can agree on
and that makes me sad

i wish i lived in a world where opinions were accepted
neighbors weren't divided
friends weren't enemies
families weren't broken

as a child everything was different
and nothing mattered
the world wasn't soft
and no one cared that much

i don't care if you are something
just don't shove it down my throat
don't attack someone just because of their look
or their culture

the land of the free
or the land of the trapped
what made us so special
that we have to involve ourselves in foriegn affairs

why can't we keep to ourselves
other than trade?
we don't need a post in every country
because is every country posted here? no.

the violence in the streets
the poverty of the communities
the struggle in which the americans face
why is there no better solution?

why can't we all get along
despite our differences?
because this place does not feel like a home
but a battlefield in wartime

let us be the country we promised our founding fathers
a united states
because the divided states
are no longer working.

OH BOY

oh boy, who lives in my dreams
tells me the world isn't as it seems
his soul so pure it gleams
his words so smooth, my interest redeems,
oh boy, never leave my dreams

oh boy, you haunt my nightmares,
although you sooth my night terrors,
i hope you can't feel my stare
i look at you and it is not fair
oh boy, you are a beautiful nightmare

oh boy, you have a beautiful soul,
i wish more people told you so,
to relieve all of your pain, that is my goal,
loved you once, i can't let go,
oh boy, you belong to my soul,

oh boy, oh boy, you are no good for me,
why does my heart see differently?
you make me blind, i cannot see,
our memories i will forever keep,
but, we both must be set free,
oh boy, why do i love you so deeply?

JUST LEAVE

my mind is at a standstill,
feeling as if it cannot go on
rushing with anger
halted at its peak

my heart is drained
emptied to the last drop
because i poured my heart out
all just for you

the easiest part of life is death
because after that is nothing
no more drama
no more disappointments

my chest aches in unrelenting pain
as my lungs tighten
because i screamed out for you
and you just left

i am at a loss
i have lost this game
for what is the point anymore
i just want to leave.

HEALING BUT BREAKING

the smell of your cologne
lingers on my cardigan
as i leave your house once again

your warm embrace is something i've longed for
for so long
and feeling it once again
made me feel more broken than ever

i don't know how i feel
about you
or about anything
you make me so conflicted

everything you are
and everything you do
is not what i want
but you are you

and for some reason
i want you

you make my head fog up
and i can't think straight
i tell you most everything
and i don't have much left to say

because of you my head is stuck
i'm high off your scent
and off the way you speak to me
but you are no good for me

and so while i struggle to heal
i am breaking
because you say you love me
but i want to break away.

TO MY HURTING HERO

when i see my loved ones hurting
there is nothing more
that i want to do
than hold them
and tell them it will be okay

one of my biggest inspirations
and motivators
is being attacked from every side
for doing her job
and teaching her students to be open minded

i wish people saw her the way i do
and if more people knew
that she saved my life
and she is the reason i am here
maybe then people would give her respect

everything she does
is from the kindness of her heart
from the selflessness of her soul
for the betterness of a future generation
for she is one of the strongest souls i know

i feel awful for her
i want to tell her it will be okay
things will improve

life will be better

but for where we are even i have a hard time believing that

i'm sorry to my hero

for the hate you get

just know i'm always here

i'm always listening

i am here because of you and for you. always.

AND YOU ARE STRONGER

there is truly nothing better
than seeing your smile again
then feeling your warm embrace
and seeing you do what you love
once again

i love seeing how
you've overcome the hatred
and are braving it out
with flying colors
you are so courageous

there is a reason i chose you
as my motivation
and greatest inspiration
because you break
and come back so much stronger

i strive to be just like you
in every way
watching you do what you love is
truly the best part of my day
thank you for being you
in every single way.

INTERSTATE

i take the interstate in hopes i'll see your car

your face

just a glimpse

to ease the pain

to scratch the itch

to soothe the tension of missing you

because in such a short time

you became my everything

to nothing once again

is this how you feel too?

THOUGHT PT.6

you saw me smiling
but i promise you
i was dying.

A STORY

there is a girl who has deep blue-eyes and dirty blonde hair

she is the average height and wears dirty white vans

she likes her eyes dark and her personality light

she shows what was the surface of a placid ocean

calm, cool, collected

every now and then thrown by a storm

the deep ocean came up and swallowed her whole

throwing her around and destroying what was once perfect

when the surface calms it sees the damage that has been done

it hides away and pushes everything away

that was this girl

from serene oceans to hidden emotions

this girl had a dream to be something big

not just something big but someone of importance

she wanted the world at her feet

she wanted to experience the street

of a city late at night with streetlights glowing

she just wanted to stare while her mind creates the story for
   her

with every light, darkness surrounds it

and when the light burned out, she could no longer see the
   light she saw darkness

and the darkness told her things she couldn't take

she was walking but heard the whispers

they were talking about her and reaching for her

if they grab her, she fears, they will take her soul and leave her
       lifeless on the side
so she signed a contract with the devil
for she is no longer free, but safe
her dreams crushed by the claws while she tries for an escape
she is isolated while the devil watches her dance like a
       monkey
she makes herself believe this is how it is supposed to be

she is trapped and cannot breathe
the devil closes in on her and she gives in
why be free when you are safe
is what he tells her
soon, he is tired of her and makes her leave
contract invalid
she is now free, but not safe
she is weak while walking back to reality
on that city street with a streetlight that is brighter than before
she stares but the whispers and claws are back
she runs with hopes of escaping
with voices screaming louder than a train
and the train is approaching fast
before the train can run her over
she wakes up, dazed and confused
her room is dark and she can't move
she feels paralyzed,
for if she moves they may get her
she thinks

this is the story of a girl who fears

a story of a girl with recurring nightmares

inked with night terrors

a girl who fights day by day to break free

because in reality, the devil still has her

and she tells no one

her oceans stay placid

her emotions stay concealed

because the contract says so

because that's what they want.

~based on a true story

I DON'T WANT TO GROW UP

i don't want to grow up

my eighteenth birthday is approaching fast
but i can't tell if i'm going to last

i don't want to grow up

adults talk about the constant struggle
life is equivalent to be being splashed with a puddle

i don't want to grow up

independence sounds like so much fun
but it really isn't like that in the long run

i don't want to grow up

it seems that the older i get
the faster the sun seems to set

i don't want to grow up

they tell me i need to slow down
but how can i when the talk of the future is all around

i don't want to grow up

why does everything seem so hard
it makes me think i will never go far

i don't want to grow up

my eyes sting with tears
the future constantly in my fears

i don't want to grow up

why does life come with so much stress?
life feels like it isn't worth living when you're this depressed

i don't want to grow up

please don't let me grow up.

SMILE

and over the years i find
that this smile has become more wide
this smile has become more kind
this smile is mine

as my mental health deteriorates
the smile that was once forced
becomes more real
i don't understand how

i wish i meant my smiles
and i wish i meant my laughs
and i as i sit here surrounded
i am so alone

i love my smile
for it is my one true pride
but it is consistently mistaken
as a true sign of happiness

the truth is
i hate smiling.

CONSISTENCY

i am so sick of being consistent
because being consistent
is being average
and being average
is not good enough

i am so sick of your inconsistency
you love me once
and one day
you decide to never love again
because i'm not good enough

i am so sick of your lack of understanding
while i know it's hard to understand
do me a favor and try
try to understand why
i feel i am not good enough

i am so sick of asking for help
help is a temporary fix
only for me to mess up again
untie the knot
because it's not tied tight enough

i am so fucking sick of being consistent
because the same habits fall back into place
and life is just average

and being consistently average

is not good enough.

GIRL IN THE MIRROR

i feel betrayed by myself

once again, i am let down

by the person who stares back at me

the girl i no longer recognize

because she decided to go and change

once again

for the pleasure of others

and by that decision

she has betrayed herself

once again.

FIRE

in the wick there is a person
and the flame is her spirit
she dances freely
in a controlled environment
and when she's pissed off
she'll burn your whole house down

she is an arsonist
on her bad days
but on her good days
she dances
and absorbs the oxygen
of the air around her

she misses her twin flame
the one that was always there
but now she dances alone
and feeds on dry air

her spirit lights up the night
as she whispers
a slight but mighty sound
and bursts her energy
to spread herself
so that she won't be so lonely

her time here is short

because we are afraid of her
no one touches her
but she wants to touch you
but she knows she'll hurt you
and that hurts her

and so at the end of the day
when we say good night
she screams and fights
and we blew out her light.

TO THOSE I HAVE HURT

i often think about the things that have hurt me
that other people have done to me
and then i think
who have i hurt?
who have i ruined?

i can think of several people
 who have made my life hard
and made me hate myself
and i remember i'm not perfect either
who have i done that to?

if it's you
i'm so sorry
sorry isn't nearly enough
but just know
i'll never forgive myself for it
and i do love you
no matter what i ever said
because who i was then
was not the best version of myself
as it isn't an excuse
i apologize for who i used to be.

BAND-AID

they say ripping off the band aid

is the easiest part

quick and smooth

and it will hurt less

damn

they were wrong again

the stinging just drags on

opening the wound back up

causing the blood to spill out

until there is nothing left.

THOUGHT: PT. 7

i keep your name on my tongue

so i feel less lonely

like the taste of your name

will sober me up

and quench my thirst

in one sip.

THE ONE THAT DIDN'T LEAVE

it's been a long time
since i've felt this content
this happy
because you have made my life
so much more enjoyable

you're so sweet
too good to be true
so polite
too kind to be real
where have you been?

you have me more confused
than any person i have ever met
yet
you have my full attention
i am intrigued by you
calm, collected
even through everything
you've been through

the closer we get,
the more i want to know everything
i want know to know your views
your whys
i want to study your eyes
and memorize them

and learn every detail of your soul

your voice
your laugh
your smile
your kindness
your passion

you are everything from
courageous to spontaneous
from passionate to compassionate
everything i look for in a person
everything seems perfect

we are the same in some ways
you and i
both humble and understanding
both insecure and awkward
in the best ways possible

you are an overall good person
and you make me feel safe
i admire your kindness
and your willingness
to be the best version of yourself
for everyone to see

i will do my best to be there for you

like you are for me
to be in your life
to help you be happier
because you deserve the world and more

you're too special for heartbreak
and too pure for hate
and too kind for this world
you are a very important person to me
and i hope you plan to stay

i can't be everything for you
and i realized that from the start
but i will try my best
to be there for you through everything

i can't be with you in any way
other than your friend
and my hope is to be best friends
because now that i have you in my life
i don't want it any other way
i can't tell if you feel the same

in every way
you are the best thing
that has come into my life so far
and i hope you stick around
for a long time

thank you for coming to my life

even if you end up leaving.

THIS FIGHT

this fight was brought on
by such petty tactics
and horrendous service to my development

it was given by anxiety
a gift from the people
who claim to be there

the inconsistency
and the clutter
brought upon my heart

you dug the trenches
deeper into my skin
and watched me suffer

your love was pure
but not sure
yet undeserving

you brought me upon your war
and expected me to fight
but not all soldiers make it home

you make me not want to come home
to your warmth
or your love

i am scared of what you offer

because this fight

is an eternal war.

8TEEN

i expect the answers be handed to me
like a gift
like on my eighteenth birthday
i'll be handed a key
a key that will unlock all secrets
and all answers
for every question i have
because as soon as adulthood strikes
everyone seems to have it figured out
and everyone seems to get it.

THE AFTERMATH

i'm not ready for the world
to open back up
to how it was
for we are so vulnerable
too raw
to face the world
once again

so why are we rushing?
must we build an immunity?
to the recklessness of the world

the world is more broken than we've ever seen
where we don't trust our neighbors
nor ourselves

and we see a picture
as the main part of life
when it has so much more to offer
and it is horrifying.

WHO AM I

a question that is asked so commonly
"who are you?"
it's a question so simple but so complex

we go our whole lives trying to find who we are
and for most, when they're found, it's too late
we spend so much time trying to figure out what we are

what are we humans?
why are humans so complicated?
sometimes i want to not be a human

i don't believe in the afterlife, but i do believe our souls are
        reincarnated
when my soul comes back,
i want to be a butterfly

i want to spread my wings and fly
i want to be recognized as beautiful
i want to live a short and sweet life

so, who am i now?
who am i in this body?
who am i in this world?

the truth is, i don't know
i feel like i am a different person than i was yesterday

figuring out who and what i am is a constant battle

life has no free trials
it is the real thing all the way around
living once in this body that was lent to your soul

at least that is how i see it
but i am constantly destroying my body
every three days

who am i?
who will i be?
what will i do?

i've learned what i love
just not how to love
myself, nor others

who, how, and what?
the questions i am constantly asking
the questions i am constantly answering
because that is who i am.

I HAVE CHANGED

i really hate when people tell me how i used to be
i used to do this
i used to say that
i used to believe in that

i don't care who i was then
or where i was then
because that is who i was then

there is a reason we have a past tense
because it is in the past
not who i am now

yes i have changed
and i am better, wiser now
i'm much better than i was

yes i have changed
i have new perspectives
some of these changes came over night
by now that shouldn't come as a shock to you

so yes i've fucking changed
and if you can't see that
you have a lot of growing up to do
maybe you need to change too.

MENTAL IMAGE

pictures are a figment of our imagination

a once-in-a-lifetime scene

a picture seen without vision

a scenery that lives in our head

you look at it once, it only lives in your head

no matter how long you stare, it'll stay in your head

unless you look back and stare and never look away

so my advice to you is to not look away

from the thing that is keeping you okay

keep your eyes from looking away

keep that mental imagine hidden away

it is easier that way.

SELF-IMAGE

i have this image of myself
that i am constantly competing for
this image of perfection
an unhealthy image
an image almost unachievable

growing up in the world i've grown up in
i feel so much pressure
to look and act a certain way
because everyone is always watching
the world is always judging
and that kills me

i want to be that girl who can go a day
eating and doing whatever i please
and be okay with that
i want to feel as if i don't have to exercise every day
eat what i want without gaining a pound
wear what i want without feeling uncomfortable

i feel as if i have to hold an image
this image i've created
but it's not me
it really isn't me

if i had it my way
i would be wearing long sleeves

and t-shirts
ripped jeans
and no skirts
because that is who i am
and how i feel.

WHERE I SEE MYSELF

the way i see myself
10 years
from now
in a little white house
covered in plants and beige walls
with wallpapers made from sheet music
and bookshelves full of
all of the poetry and
all of the best books
and a room with my vinyls
and my record player
playing non stop throughout the day
and posters plastering my bedroom wall
of all the things i loved before
i can see the sun shining
through the pale curtains
and a basket full of every fruit
in every room

outside my window i see mountains
the most beautiful view
with the valleys and
the snowy tips
all their rough and sharp edges
and smooth streams and soft trees

and i can see myself

oversized cardigans
and white t shirts
at a desk
writing my next novel
wearing my clear glasses
with my head shaved
and a cup of iced coffee
and after all this time
i am happy.

the only thing i fail to see
is who i am with
who i am loving
who i am longing for
i can see myself ending up alone
but is that what i want?
what if it is not a choice
what if i am seeing myself happy
but again it is a face
as i am doing at this moment?

what really changes in 10 years?
and why do i see this version of myself?
this is where i want to be
but at what cost?

MIND GAMES

i could spend hours in my head
playing games,
thinking things,
sometimes it's not that bad

sometimes my mind tells
stories
twisted tales
frightening fantasies
mind filled with
never-ending glories

there is a radio in my brain
extended collection
adjustable volume
but the same songs play over and over again

i can see pictures in my head
high quality
dipping colors
vivid movies with every word said

my mind holds a museum
historical features
creepy creatures
how i wish i could show you them

i have voices that speak to me

mean voices

calm voices

these voices have a hard time agreeing

my brain is a world

with rules and regulations

with wonder and awe

it in itself is a game.

IT IS OKAY TO HAVE A GOOD DAY

the kind of anxiety i have
is the self deprecating one
the self harmful one
the one that makes it hard to have a good day

i always hear and read the words
"its okay to have a bad day"
but i never see
"its okay to have a good day"
because that's not what my mind
tells me

it tells me that every day sucks
and that i am
undeserving
of a good day

the voice in my head says
i can't have a good day
even if it was a good day
something has to ruin it.

THOUGHT: PT. 8

i've isolated myself
to prepare for the worst
so the hurt won't be so much
so it will be a little bit easier when i go.

SLIPPING THROUGH YOUR FINGERS ALL THE TIME

warm and smooth
like my mothers hand
walking through the mall
at 5 years old
looking upon every store in wonder
searching and exploring
like this large place is empty
and it's just me
and my mother

i've always envied my mother
her perfect white teeth
her shining personality
her ability to still be in one piece
even after everything she's been through

mother, i know you're reading this
and i know you're seeing me
and i know you love me more than anything
i'm sorry i don't reciprocate those feelings
out loud and in the open

in my head i'm screaming
into a valley that echos
tears burning as they rolls down my cheeks
"i love you," i scream
but the words never come out

they're trapped in my throat
much like i feel trapped in this place
and it's not that i want to leave you, mother
for a new place or a new life
but to be independent

you've done so much for me
and while i may not seem grateful
because i haven't quite figured out
how to display my feelings in such ways
i am nothing but indebted to you
your sacrifices and your love
it feels unworthy to me
because what have i done for you?
it only makes me feel guilty

i don't know everything, i admit
i'm not as wise or knowledgeable as you
but i see the world through a different lens
a lens that is different from yours
and that is okay
we're different, mother
yet exactly the same

one day i will figure out how to repay you
how to shower you with appreciation
and believe me when i say
i'm constantly working on it

but like with everything
it takes time

give me time, mother
i need time to grieve
the little girl that used to be
holding your hand
give me time to learn to let go
and try to be free.

MIND

it isn't a secret that my mind is always wondering

i have said more times in my writing than one can count

it's always "my mind this" and "my mind that"

i give my brain too much credit

but wait

didn't my brain just write that?

didn't my brain just think of that?

that's the weird thing about brains

that is all you are

we are all walking brains

our brain is our best friend

our brain is our worst enemy

brain is us

i am weirdly aware of my brain

i am aware of so many things happening around me

i am aware of the brainwashed people

thinking this life is what it seems

we live in a world of materials

that are a figment of our imagination

my mind moves at light speed

random thoughts constantly

and i often wonder why things happen

how they happen

why our brain makes or breaks us

is the world what it seems?

are things only here because we're told they are?

is the world really real?

can you tell i wholeheartedly believe in the matrix?

QUESTIONING THE NORMAL

a younger student once told me

that writing is what you make it to be

and i have never agreed more

writing should not have rules

as he said

but it should be a freedom

of expression

without the grammar

or punctuation

because life

is way too short

to be worried about

little things like that

-said the future english teacher.

THE VISITATION

visitations are sometimes sickening
with the widowed wife staring
her eyes damp putting on a strong face
greeting the others
to look at her deceased husband's body
laying in a wooden box
a soulless, lifeless body
laying as still as a rock
while others pass by and pat their eyes

in a room full of people socializing
recalling the events of the life
that no longer exists in this room
the body white
no longer existing
just waiting to be put in the earth

the widowed wife cries as every person approaches her
with hugs and "he's no longer in pain" statements
and condolences given
too many times
in this room full of people who are full of life
with this one person whose body is left in a box
alone until the end of time.

THE FUNERAL

soon we gather in a place
a place full of dead bodies rotting in the ground
all in their final resting place
with stones above them only displaying their beginnings and
endings

and in this place we say goodbye
to the body that was once full of life
but life was sucked from it
a tragic ending
to a beautiful life

prayers are said
tears are cried
like a leaking faucet
or a burst pipe
and we say goodbye.

BREATHE

i used to let the world consume me

much like water consumes my being

in a deep swimming pool

filling my pores

soaking up every drop

making me heavier

resulting in me sinking

like an anchor

trapped searching for air

but unable to reach the surface

the feeling of the world crushing me

as each event digs deeper

my heart refuses to strengthen itself

but anymore

i've taught myself to swim

to take myself out of the mess

to allow myself to no longer

be subject to the suffering

but to come above the water

to breathe

with practice and patience

slowly again

my lungs are filled with air

sweet, soothing air

no longer trapped under the rubble

of the world's problems.

CELL PHONE

addiction is a hell of a thing
everyone has one
whether they know it or not
almost no one can live without
the little rectangle
that supplies
all of the knowledge
anyone can ever dream of

i often wonder what life would be like
without this tool
would i be happier?
would the world be less divided?
would life be better?
the media makes it worse
and scrolling constantly
makes me truly want to end it all

i am guilty of being addicted
i've had times when my phone has been my best friend
when scrolling was the only comfort i've had
but after i feel guilty
like i've wasted my time
the hours spent on my phone
are hours of my life gone
and i often remember that
and i feel so guilty

i don't to be put in a group
obsessed with phones
because i really am not
i do my best to stay away from it
it is hard sometimes
but i'm working on it

i wish that because i try to break myself from the habit
i wouldn't be made fun of
or called lame
or anything else
i wish i was considered better
than the average teenager
like my age defines my personality
it really doesn't
i'm pretty sure of who i am
and what i believe in

at eighteen years old
i have learned so much already
i know how to care for myself
and what i can handle
when to ask for help
and when to take a step back
every day i remind myself
that i don't need my phone
it is simply a privilege

and i don't want to spend another minute

wasting my time looking at things

that don't even matter

and make me angry or upset

social media sucks

especially now

and it's suffocating

i can't breathe thinking about it

i'm trapped in this world

that lives on a 5 inch screen

and i'm missing the beauty of the real world

take me back

to when cell phones were plastic

and sang songs

to when scrolling through pictures

meant going through old photo albums

to when following and unfollowing people

didn't define a friendship

the world is so toxic

and i hate living in it.

FEELING PRETTY

unsure of what constitutes the meaning of "pretty"
but certainly sure of the meaning
society has created for it

father doesn't like girls with short hair
and mother laughs at boys with long hair
because neither of those
fits the definition of their sexual gender
they are not seen as "pretty"

it's hard to feel pretty
when looking at the same face
each day when waking up
finding a new flaw
unearthing a new scar
crying looking at the face
of the one thing life is spent with
the body

it is told that pretty is not
acne-covered faces
teeth fixed by braces
too little or too much weight
slouching over or sitting up straight

brought upon the minds of humans
of a perfect human

every human strives to be
but are utterly disappointed
when perfect is as it seems

the world is full of beautiful people
with ugly insides
swamped with
judgment, ideals, selfishness
why can't the definition of pretty
be more than just a face?
more than just a body?

the whole world is fixated on one thing
perfection
when it really ceases to exist.

WRITE, WRITE, WRITE!

from the time i was in first grade,
i've been told i have talent for writing
for creating
for thinking.

i always enjoyed writing,
it is amazing how a whole page can be
a representation of the mind

this book is my mind written out

i've practiced depth
i've practiced metaphors
i've practiced visualization
with my words

writing helps me understand
it helps me realize
what is really going on

my writing is what my mind is indirectly telling me

poetry is my favorite genre of writing
especially free verse
there is something so beautiful about
pieces with a world of emotions
without a rhythmic criteria

ever since my first therapy appointments
they've been telling me to write
saying it will help

and i hate to admit, they were right.

painting a picture with words
that is my goal
i want to see the story
rather than read it

i want to write, write, write!
for the rest of my life.

CONCLUDING THOUGHTS

this is where it ends

there are so many things i have left to say
but i will leave them for another time and place

while my embers will keep burning
i leave this as my peace offering
in hopes the embers will fade

i have so many dreams
and so many hopes
and i hope for the world
that my words have helped

my thoughts and opinions
are controversial
i hope they made sense
i hope you found some comfort
even if it's just a little bit

just a reminder that your embers are not permanent
they will fade
you can make it through another day
another week
another month
another year
and you will be okay

thank you for coming with me
on this journey
of self growth
and helping me
cope with my embers
for me, always remember

it will be okay eventually.

ABOUT THE AUTHOR

Abi is an aspiring poet and future teacher from rural Illinois. Her love for poetry started at a young age, and it has been her dream to be published before graduation. She plans to continue to share her stories through writing and her passion for literature through teaching. Her experience with mental health has led her down a path to help others in their own journeys.

Abi will be attending Drake University in Des Moines, IA to pursue her career in education.

Photo by: Infinity Photography

SOCIALS
Twitter: poetabix_
Instagram: poetabix

mental health matters.
self-love and healing matters
love yourself like you love others.
promise me: you will never give up

if you or a loved one is suffering from mental health, self harm, anxiety, depression, suicidal thoughts, etc. visit this website https://suicidepreventionlifeline.org or call 800-273-8255.

if you are a victim of sexual assault and need support, visit this website https://www.rainn.org or call 1-800-656-4673

SOME IMPORTANT AWARENESS MONTHS CORRELATING TO THESE TOPICS:
March is National Self-Injury Awareness Month
April is National Sexual Assault Awareness Month
May is National Mental Health Awareness Month
September is National Suicide Awareness Month

i love you. always and forever.